# KOBE BRYANT

## A League Of His Own

### WHAT IT TAKES TO BE LIKE KOBE

*An Unauthorized Biography*

By Steve James

Copyright© 2016 by Steve James - All rights reserved.

**Copyright**: No part of this publication may be reproduced without written permission from the author, except by a reviewer who may quote brief passages or reproduce illustrations in a review with appropriate credits; nor may any part of this book be reproduced, stored in a retrieval system, or transmitted in any form or by any means – electronic, mechanical, photocopying, recording, or other – without prior written permission of the copyright holder.

**Disclaimer**: The following book is for entertainment or informational purposes only. The information in this book is true and complete to the best of our knowledge. All recommendations are made without guarantee on the part of the author. It is solely the reader's responsibility to check all information contained in this book before relying upon it. Neither the author nor publisher can be held accountable for any errors or omissions. The author disclaims any liability in connection with the use of this information. References are provided for informational purposes only and do not constitute endorsement of any websites or other sources. Readers should be aware that the websites listed in this book may change.

This book is not intended as legal or medical advice. If any such specialized advice is needed, seek a qualified individual to help.

The trademarks are used without any consent, and the publication of the trademark is without permission or backing by the trademark owner. All trademarks and brands within this book are for clarifying purposes only with no intent to infringe on the trademark owners.

This book is not sponsored by or affiliated with the National Basketball Association, its teams, the players, or anyone involved with them.

First Printing, 2016 - Printed in the United States of America

*"If you don't believe in yourself, no one will do it for you."*

- Kobe Bryant

# TABLE OF CONTENTS

| | |
|---|---|
| Introduction | 1 |
| Chapter 1 – Upbringing | 3 |
| Chapter 2 – High School Years | 5 |
| Chapter 3 – Professional NBA Career | 9 |
| Chapter 4 – International Basketball | 37 |
| Chapter 5 – Exclusive Drills and Exercises Used by Kobe Bryant | 39 |
|    Strength Training | 40 |
|    Basketball Drills | 47 |
|    Defensive Drills | 51 |
| Chapter 6 – Personal Life, Business, and Philanthropy | 53 |
| Chapter 7 – His Fears and Superstitions | 61 |
| Chapter 8 – Top 8 Motivational Lessons from Kobe Bryant | 65 |
| Chapter 9 – Famous People Inspired by Kobe | 67 |
| Chapter 10 – Kobe's Basketball Philosophy | 69 |
| Chapter 11 – 15 Interesting Facts You Didn't Know About Kobe Bryant | 73 |
| Chapter 12 – Awards and Recognition | 77 |
| Chapter 13 – NBA Season Stats | 83 |
| Conclusion | 85 |
| About the Author | 87 |

# INTRODUCTION

It's 4:00 a.m. and his alarm goes off. Kobe rolls out of bed, brushes his teeth quickly, puts on his clothes, and heads out the door.

The team practice is not until 11:00 a.m., but he wants to get in a few extra *hours* of work first. By 5:00 a.m., he is sweating profusely. By 6:00, he's already done tons of sprints and has sunk 100 shots. This is about a fifth of what he'll make most days.

This is, and has been, **the life and work ethic of Kobe Bryant.**

Kobe entered the NBA straight out of high school, and comparisons between him and Michael Jordan permeated the media. The teenager was cast off by many as arrogant, unappreciative, and cocky, and his private lifestyle did little to aid in his relationship both with his teammates and the public early on. But this is a guy who has spent over half of his life in the NBA, and his entire life undeniably devoted to the sport.

In this book, we'll take a comprehensive look at Kobe's life and examine **how and why he became the legend that he already is today.** We'll take a look at his trajectory – both as a person and as an athlete. We'll delve into his training regimens and see how his constant work ethic has translated to success. And we'll deeply analyze his mind-set. We'll learn how he has developed the mentality that he has toward training, the public, failures and successes, motivations, etc.

**Kobe is unlike anyone else!** He is an enigmatic creature, who, despite over twenty years in the public eye, is poorly understood. He has strings of DNA that most people do not possess, and he has a work ethic that most people cannot develop, no matter how hard they try.

*Who is Kobe, really?* This book seeks to find out.

# CHAPTER 1
# UPBRINGING

Kobe was born on August 23, 1978, into a basketball family. He had two older siblings, and he was named after the Japanese Kobe beef. His father's nickname, 'jellybean,' is the origin for Kobe's middle name 'Bean.' His father, Joe Bryant, was a graduate of La Salle University and would go on to play for the Philadelphia 76ers for four seasons alongside Julius Erving, Doug Collins, and George McGinnis. He then played from 1980-1982 for the San Diego Clippers and concluded his NBA career in Houston with the Rockets in 1983.

When Kobe was just three years old, he started playing basketball. Joe moved the family to Italy to continue playing in the Italian A1 and A2 leagues, where Kobe was initially raised. Thus, Italian was his first language, and he still speaks it fluently today. However, during the summers, the family would come to the United States and Kobe played in the Sonny Hill League in Philadelphia.

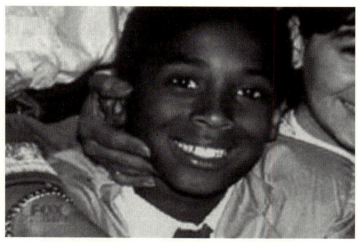

Kobe and his father would watch videos of Joe's games and study them together. He also **studied the games of Magic Johnson and Michael Jordan** growing up – two players he admired, along with football player, Emmitt Smith. Kobe also attended many of Joe's practices and games. He would try to mimic his father's moves, even during halftime of some of his father's games. Growing up in Italy, however, where soccer was king, many urged Kobe to put his athletic talents on the soccer field. Though he played growing up, his passion was always centered on basketball.

In 1991-1992, Joe began playing for a team in France. This took a toll on Kobe and his sisters. They had to commute two hours to their international school in Switzerland every day. After the exhausting year, Joe and Pam decided it was time to move their kids back to the United States for school.

When Joe decided his playing career was over, the family returned back to Pennsylvania in the early 1990s. Joe began coaching the women's varsity team in Lower Merion, Pennsylvania, at the Akiba Hebrew Academy. After one season, Joe took an assistant coaching position at La Salle University. Finally in 2005, he received an offer from the WNBA to coach the Los Angeles Sparks. After two years, he was replaced. He has since coached teams in Japan, Italy, and Thailand.

# CHAPTER 2
# HIGH SCHOOL YEARS

After a productive summer of training, Kobe made the varsity basketball team at Lower Merion High School in Ardmore, Pennsylvania as a freshman. This was a rare occurrence at such a large school, and he was **the first freshman in many years to make the starting lineup for the Aces**.

His first year, the team did poorly, winning only 4 of 24 games. However, Bryant would soon begin to change the team dynamic. Throughout his first two years of high school, Kobe was also adapting to the American way of teenage life. He managed to maintain a B average in his grades, but making friends was a different challenge.

Kobe really came into his own form during his junior year. He was 6'5" and realized that if he wanted to pursue a professional career in basketball, he would need to **start training like a guard**. Coach Gregg Downer encouraged this development, as the mismatches Kobe faced proved beneficial for the team. No one could defend him, and he averaged 31.1 points, 10.4 rebounds, and 5.2 assists per game, earning him the title of ***Pennsylvania Player of the Year.*** The team did well and made it to the state playoffs but were knocked out in the semi-finals. He was devastated and told his teammates:

*"Next time we stop playing basketball, it's because there's no games left."*

Kobe's father was undoubtedly instrumental in his development. He knew strategies and tricks that high school players simply did not know – how to pinch people when getting a rebound, how to flop successively. During games, his father would even yell out instructions in Italian so no one else could understand, which Kobe would follow successfully.

After such an impressive year, nearly every big college program in the country was eager to sell their program to Kobe. His good grades and high SAT scores made Duke, North Carolina, Villanova, and Michigan some of the top contenders. **Kobe was on top of the high school sporting world**, but his potential future plans only expanded when he witnessed Kevin Garnett getting chosen first in the 1995 NBA Draft, right out of high school.

During the summer between his junior and senior year, Joe was able to strike a deal with the 76ers, allowing Kobe to work out with some members of the team. Although he had work to do, it was evident that he would soon be able to keep up with NBA players. That summer, he also attended ***the Adidas ABCD camp,*** **where he earned the MVP** and further impressed scouts and coaches.

During his senior year, Kobe led the Aces to a 31-3 record and state championship title – their first in fifty-three years. Fans, college coaches, and scouts filled the stands for every game. The team was also invited to participate in a number of significant tournaments. The end of the year revealed these averages: 30.8 points, 4.0 steals, 3.8 blocked shots. **Kobe was designated Southeast Pennsylvania's all-time lead scorer, totalling 2,883 career points.**

At this point, Kobe Bryant had become a household name. There was endless chatter as to whether or not Kobe would transition straight into the NBA. He had already gained the reputation of being a cocky young man, and stunts like taking Brandy, popular R&B singer, to the prom only propagated these perceptions.

Finally, Kobe held a press conference in the Lower Merion gym, and alongside friends from *Boyz II Men,* **he announced that he would enter the NBA draft.** While many sportswriters believed Kobe was ready for the jump, others personally criticized his family for encouraging such a big leap. He wore sunglasses, and as he was about to announce he was taking his talents to the NBA, he paused as if he forgot. Many people considered the event and presentation arrogant, which would come to define his image in the coming years.

# STEVE JAMES

# CHAPTER 3
# PROFESSIONAL NBA CAREER

## DRAFT

Kobe entered the 1996 NBA Draft in the same year as Marcus Camby, Allen Iverson, Stephon Marbury, and Ray Allen. Thus, any thoughts of being selected first, despite his overwhelming amount of talent, were soon dismissed. The Los Angeles Lakers, with president Jerry West, were very interested in Kobe. They even held a private workout with him to evaluate his athletic ability as well as fundamental skills.

On the day of the draft, the **Charlotte Hornets drafted Kobe with the 13th pick**. The Lakers picked up Derek Fisher in the first round as their 24th pick. West, savvy as he is, **arranged a trade for Kobe**, letting go of their big man, Vlade Divac. After the trade, the Lakers had money to spare and were able to sign Shaquille O'Neal, who had just become a free agent after playing for the Orlando Magic. In what seemed like a matter of minutes, the soon-to-be dynasty was created. Because Kobe was only seventeen at the time of the daft, his parents had to co-sign his contract of $3.5 million for three years.

The media were very critical of his decision to go directly to the NBA. Articles ran saying that he was delusional and making stupid decisions. However, what the assistant coaches in the NBA and other players said about him, was that he was well beyond his years. Having a father who played basketball professionally, he knew what to expect. Behind closed doors, the Lakers interviewed him long before the draft, and he showed poise and reasonable reasons for his jump.

## 1996-1997 Rookie Season

Despite averaging 25 points per game during the summer league, **during his first year in the NBA, Kobe did not usually start**. He often came off the bench to give relief to guards Eddie Jones and Nick Van Exel. By the end of his first year, he averaged only 15.5 minutes and 7.6 points per game.

However, he got a glimpse of fame at the *1997 Slam Dunk Contest* during All-Star Weekend. At only eighteen years old, **he became the youngest player to ever win the contest**.

The Lakers made the playoffs in his first year, but **Bryant was criticized for his end-of-the-game shots**. He finished the season with four air balls and missed a game winning shot against the Utah Jazz.

Socially and mentally, Kobe struggled. Having been raised abroad and moving around so much, he was not used to having long-term friendships. Further, he was so much younger than his teammates, and they had very little in common. During his first few years in the NBA, he had a hard time making friends and forming trusting relationships with his teammates.

## 1997-1998 Season

In Kobe's second year, he began to see much more court time as the designated sixth man. He averaged between 20-30 minutes and 15.4 points per game, essentially doubling his previous season averages. In addition to winning the ***NBA's Sixth Man of the Year Award***, he became **the youngest**

**player to start at the All-Star Game**. He also got to play alongside three of his teammates – O'Neal, Van Exel, and Jones.

Kobe's performance and attitude at the All-Star Game came under great scrutiny. The media had boasted that the matchup was one between Jordan and Kobe, a thread that had narrated Kobe's entrance into the NBA. Kobe reacted rashly, playing selfishly, and criticizing Karl Malone. He ended up being benched for the entire fourth quarter.

Many continued to **criticize Kobe for hogging the ball** as the season progressed. When they finally started playing Kobe less, the message began to sink in. The team made it to the Western Conference Finals, only to be knocked out again by the Jazz.

## 1998-1999 Season

A lockout postponed the start of the shortened 1998-1999 season, and the Lakers were able to sign Dennis Rodman, promote assistant coach Kurt Rambis to head, and trade to obtain Glen Rice, J.R. Reid, and B.J. Armstrong. This would be the perfect supporting cast for a growing Kobe Bryant.

Now a starter, Kobe averaged 19.9 points per game, and had 9 double-doubles during the season. Despite finishing with a confidence-boosting 31-19 record, the Lakers lost to the Spurs in a second-round 4-game sweep. **The media continued testing Kobe** by publishing rumors that O'Neal was jealous of Kobe, that Kobe was rude and cocky, etc. The result was bringing ***Phil Jackson on board as the head coach***.

## A New Lakers Era 1999-2000 Season

Jackson brought with him to the Lakers a triangle offense, which he successfully employed for winning six championships while playing for the Chicago Bulls. The offensive strategy was used to bring out both the best in Bryant and O'Neal. Although Kobe missed a few weeks due to injury, he came back averaging 38 minutes per game.

The Lakers ended the regular season with 67 wins and 15 losses, and Kobe seemed to have improved tenfold. Further, he and O'Neal were finally truly playing like teammates. Los Angeles moved past the Sacramento Kings in the first round and the Phoenix Suns in the second round to face the Portland Trailblazers in the Western Conference Finals. In Game 7, they came back from a 13-point deficit to finally make it to the NBA Finals.

Jalen Rose intentionally put his foot below Kobe as Kobe was up in the air to cause an injury. It worked, as Kobe rolled his ankle and missed most of Game 2 and all of Game 3. However, in Game 4, he came back strong, scoring 22 points in the second half and scoring a game winning shot in overtime to win the game. A 116-111 Game 6 victory became **Kobe's first ever NBA championship** and the Lakers' first since 1988.

## 2000-2001 Season

Although Kobe averaged 28.5 points per game, more than the preceding year, the Lakers won 56 games, 11 fewer than the previous year. Despite this, their playoff record was 15-1.

They cruised past all the Western Conference teams and faced the Philadelphia 76ers in the finals. Kobe averaged 29.4 points, 7.3 rebounds, and 6.1 assists per game in the post season. **The Lakers won the NBA championship** for the second year in a row.

## Kobe-Shaq Drama

Even as the Lakers were successful, there was tension between the two superstars. Kobe, a serious and determined player, and Shaq, a bubbly and playful personality, did not mesh well. Shaq even held a meeting at one point saying that the team was incapable of winning with Kobe.

Kobe, in general, was somewhat isolated from the rest of the team. His ultra-competitive attitude made some of the teammates question his motives. Ultimately, Kobe reconciled the differences between both Shaq and the rest of the team.

# Three-Peat 2001-2002 Season

Although Kobe's averages slightly dropped in the 2001-2002 season, he played 80 games and shot 46.9% from the field. In addition to winning the **All-Star MVP** trophy, he also made the **All-NBA Defensive team** and the **All-NBA First team**.

Although the Lakers did not cruise to the finals unscathed like the previous year, they were able to surpass all the Western opponents to face off against the New Jersey Nets. In the series, Kobe had averages of 26.8 points, 5.8 rebounds, and 5.3 assists per game, while shooting over 50% from the field. He delivered strong performances in the final minutes, establishing himself as a go-to player.

## 2002-2003 Season

Heading into the 2002-2003 season, the Lakers had the championship to lose. Kobe played well, averaging 30 points, 6.9 rebounds, 5.9 assists, and 2.2 steals per game, scoring over 40 points in 9 consecutive games, and setting the NBA record for 3-point goals in one game (making 12 against the Super Sonics).

The Lakers finished the season with a 50-32 record and made it through the round of the playoffs. However, they lost to the San Antonio Spurs in the Western Conference semi-finals in 6 games.

## 2003-2004 Season

After signing Karl Malone and Gary Payton the following year, the Lakers were very threatening again. However, the season coincided with Kobe being arrested for sexual assault (this is mentioned in detail later on). This not only cast an intensely negative spotlight on both himself and the team, but he was also absent from games due to court appearances.

For the season's final game, the Lakers met the Portland Trail Blazers. Bryant made a statement to fans and the world when he hit a game tying shot with 1.1 seconds in the fourth quarter to send the game into overtime. He then hit a 3-pointer at the buzzer to win 105-104 in overtime.

The Lakers cruised through the playoffs to play the Detroit Pistons in the NBA Finals. Kobe's averages of 22.6 points and 4.4 assists per game were not enough as the Pistons won the series.

## 2004-2005 Season

At the end of 2004, the **Lakers saw many changes**. Shaq got traded to the Miami Heat in exchange for Brian Grant, Caron Butler, and Lamar Odom. Rudy Tomjanovich stepped up when Phil Jackson's contract wasn't renewed. Kobe's contract, too, was up, but he re-signed for another seven years with the Lakers.

Media scrutiny for Kobe was possibly worse than ever following the dismissal of the rape case. Phil Jackson also published a book about the previous season where he called Kobe an *"un-coachable" player*. Tomjanovich would also step out, and the Lakers would play under Frank Hamblen.

Kobe managed to average 27.6 points per game, becoming the league's second leading scorer, but it was no doubt **the most disappointing season** of his career up until that point. The team went 34-48 and failed to make the playoffs.

## 2005-2006 Season

Surprisingly, Phil Jackson returned to the Lakers for 2005-2006. This season, **Kobe would put up incredible individual performances** that simply no other player in the NBA could replicate. He scored 62 points in just three quarters playing against the Dallas Mavericks in December 2005. He even went so far as to outscore the entire team 62-61.

Then, **Bryant scored 81 points** playing against the Toronto Raptors in January 2006. In this performance, he broke the franchise record and became the player with **the second-highest total in NBA history**. Wilt Chamberlain remains the first player, after scoring 100 points in 1962.

After this, Kobe was given the nickname *"The Black Mamba"* because of his 'deadly' scoring capability. Around this time, Kobe and Mark Jackson also coined the phrase *"Momma there goes that man again."*

The Lakers' record improved, finishing the season with 45 wins and 37 losses. The Lakers faced off against the Phoenix Suns, led by that year's MVP Steve Nash. Despite going up 3-1, the Suns rallied back and won the series in 7 games.

# 2006-2007 Season

After knee surgery, Kobe entered the next season with a new knee and new number – 24 (more on this later). Kobe faced a number of issues on the court. He was suspended for an elbow to the face with Manu Ginobili. This happened twice more in a short period of time – he was suspended for elbowing Marko Jaric and given a flagrant foul for elbowing Kyle Korver. These incidents began to earn Kobe a **reputation for playing dirty**.

Kobe finished the year with high point-scoring performances. He had ten 50-plus performances, three of which were consecutive. **He again won the league's scoring title** and his new jersey was the top-selling jersey from the NBA in China and the U.S. However, the Suns defeated the Lakers in the first round again, this time in a more dominant 4-1 fashion.

## 2007-2008 Season

Behind the scenes, although not un-public, there was tension heading into the next season. Kobe went back and forth publicly stating that he wanted to be traded. However, on the court, things were hardly rough.

In December, **he reached 20,000 points, becoming the youngest player to do so**. He also displayed a rarely seen physical toughness. On his shooting hand, he injured the MCP joint in one of his fingers, suffered an avulsion fracture, and tore the radical collateral ligament. He played all 82 games despite the injury, postponing surgery to the end of the season. Ultimately, he ended up not having the surgery.

The signing of Pau Gasol would help bring the Lakers back to their old form. They finished the regular season with a 57-25 record. They swept the Nuggets in the first round of the playoffs, and Kobe posted several 30-plus performances to get past the Utah Jazz in the next round. The Lakers beat the San Antonio Spurs to win the Western Conference Finals and would play the Boston Celtics in the finals – a classic matchup. The Celtics had just brought in Kevin Garnett and Ray Allen to join Paul Pierce. However, despite making it so far, the Celtics surpassed the Lakers in 6 games.

Kobe finally won the **NBA MVP award**. In his speech, he showed a great deal of poise and perspective.

## 2008-2009 Season

The Lakers opened the 2008-2009 season with a bang. They began with a 21-3 record, and Kobe was doing his thing. He scored 61 points against the New York Knicks and 27 points in the All-Star Game. He and Shaquille O'Neal jointly shared the title of **All-Star Game MVP**.

The Lakers more or less cruised past the Western conference contenders in the playoffs to again make it to the finals to play the Orlando Magic. They won the series in 5 games, and Kobe won the **NBA Finals MVP**. In the series, he averaged 32.4 points, 7.4 assists, 5.6 rebounds, 1.4 steals, and 1.4 blocks.

## 2009-2010 Season

Kobe again injured his finger early in the 2009-2010 season. And again, he opted to play hurt. He seemed to be on fire, with high scoring performances and game winning shots. Shortly after reaching the mark of 25,000 points, he passed Jerry West and became **the all-time leading scorer in franchise history**.

Kobe missed 9 games due to injuries in the season, but signed a 3-year contract extension for $87 million, nonetheless. Again, the Lakers made it to the championship in a rematch against the Celtics. It was an exciting 7-game series, which the Lakers ended up winning. Kobe won the ***NBA Finals MVP*** for the second consecutive year and declared it his most satisfying championship.

## 2010-2011 Season

Despite averaging less than 20 shots a game in the 2010-2011 season, Kobe moved up to the *6th spot on the list of NBA all-time scorers*.

Kobe found himself in a **negative spotlight yet again**; this time, for yelling a gay slur to a referee. The NBA fined him $100,000, but more damaging was the criticism from the Gay & Lesbian Alliance Against Defamation. He publicly apologized for the slip-up, and the Lakers publicly criticized him as well.

The team did not advance past the second round of the playoffs after the Dallas Mavericks handed them a serious defeat.

## 2011-2012 Season

Heading into the next season, Phil Jackson retired and Kobe was treating numerous injuries. However, Kobe put up a number of stunning performances scoring over 40 points.

That said, throughout the season injuries kept coming – a broken nose, a bruised shin, etc. After missing several games, he came back to join the Lakers in the playoffs, but they were knocked out by the young Oklahoma City Thunder, led by Kevin Durant.

## 2012-2013 Season

Hope came in the form of Dwight Howard and Steve Nash in the following season. In November, Kobe's 1,725th steal put him ahead of Magic Johnson for the **all-time leader in steals**. **Bryant also scored 30,000 points** a few weeks later, joining a club with members Michael Jordan, Wilt Chamberlain, Karl Malone, and Kareem Abdul-Jabbar.

Kobe also played an important role on defense. New coach, Mike D'Antoni, frequently had the well-conditioned Kobe guarding the best perimeter players. He also began racking up more assists as he expanded his in-game skills. However, things would come to a screeching halt in April when he tore his Achilles tendon. Even at thirty-four years old, he was playing over 38 minutes a game, trying to get his team into the playoffs. His season ended early as he headed into surgery and recovery.

## 2013-2014 Season

Having faced numerous injuries, people were skeptical when Kobe signed a 2-year contract extension for $48.5 million. His loyalty to the Lakers was noted, as he would be the first NBA player ever (soon) to play twenty years with the same franchise. However, criticism arose as he was still the highest paid player in the league, despite his fragility. People brought up issues relating to the fact that his huge salary limited opportunities for the Lakers to get other potentially strong players.

More injuries sidelined him for weeks throughout the season. Despite being selected for the All-Star Game, he did not play, and openly admitted he was not deserving of the spot. By March, having come in and out of play, he opted to sit out the remainder of the season as the Lakers finished with a disappointing 27-55 record.

## 2014-2015 Season

Kobe was allegedly healthy entering the 2014-2015 season. In November he recorded a triple double – his 20th. Later, he became t**he NBA's 3rd all-time leading scorer with 32,292 points**. After experiencing soreness in a range of areas, Bryant sat out for a number of games.

Yet again, his season ended in injury. In January he tore his rotator cuff and needed surgery to recover.

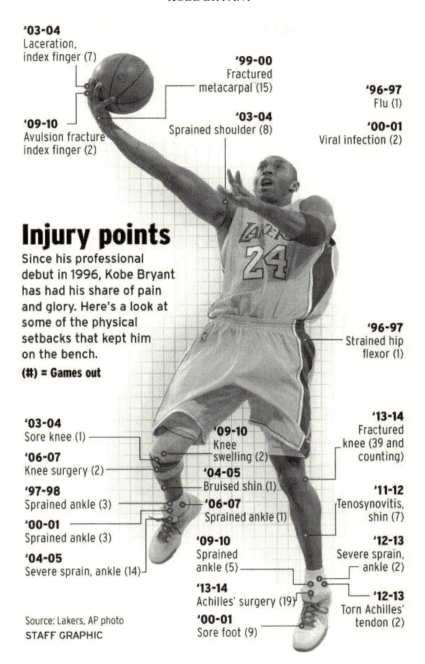

## Injury points

Since his professional debut in 1996, Kobe Bryant has had his share of pain and glory. Here's a look at some of the physical setbacks that kept him on the bench.

**(#) = Games out**

'03-04 Laceration, index finger (7)
'09-10 Avulsion fracture index finger (2)
'99-00 Fractured metacarpal (15)
'03-04 Sprained shoulder (8)
'96-97 Flu (1)
'00-01 Viral infection (2)
'96-97 Strained hip flexor (1)
'03-04 Sore knee (1)
'06-07 Knee surgery (2)
'97-98 Sprained ankle (3)
'00-01 Sprained ankle (3)
'04-05 Severe sprain, ankle (14)
'09-10 Knee swelling (2)
'04-05 Bruised shin (1)
'06-07 Sprained ankle (1)
'09-10 Sprained ankle (5)
'13-14 Achilles' surgery (19)
'00-01 Sore foot (9)
'13-14 Fractured knee (39 and counting)
'11-12 Tenosynovitis, shin (7)
'12-13 Severe sprain, ankle (2)
'12-13 Torn Achilles' tendon (2)

Source: Lakers, AP photo
STAFF GRAPHIC

# 2015-2016 Season

Kobe played in the 2015-2016 season opener, his 20th season with the Lakers.

On November 29, 2015, **Kobe announced his retirement at the end of the 2015-2016 season**, in the form of a poem:

*Dear Basketball,*
*From the moment*
*I started rolling my dad's tube socks*
*And shooting imaginary*
*Game-winning shots*
*In the Great Western Forum*
*I knew one thing was real*
*I fell in love with you.*

*A love so deep I gave you my all —*
*From my mind & body*
*To my spirit & soul.*

## KOBE BRYANT

*As a six-year-old boy*
*Deeply in love with you*
*I never saw the end of the tunnel.*
*I only saw myself*
*Running out of one.*
*And so I ran.*

*I ran up and down every court*
*After every loose ball for you.*
*You asked for my hustle*
*I gave you my heart*
*Because it came with so much more.*

*I played through the sweat and hurt*
*Not because challenge called me*
*But because YOU called me.*
*I did everything for YOU*
*Because that's what you do*
*When someone makes you feel as*
*Alive as you've made me feel.*

*You gave a six-year-old boy his Lakers dream*
*And I'll always love you for it.*
*But I can't love you obsessively for much longer.*
*This season is all I have left to give.*
*My heart can take the pounding*
*My mind can handle the grind*
*But my body knows it's time to say goodbye.*

*And that's OK.*
*I'm ready to let you go.*
*I want you to know now*
*So we both can savor every moment we have left together.*
*The good and the bad.*
*We have given each other*
*All that we have.*

*And we both know, no matter what I do next*
*I'll always be that kid*
*With the rolled up socks*
*Garbage can in the corner*
*:05 seconds on the clock*
*Ball in my hands.*
*5 ... 4 ... 3 ... 2 ... 1*

*Love you always,*
*Kobe*

## STEVE JAMES

His final NBA game took place at home at Staples Center against the Utah Jazz on Wednesday, April 13, 2016.

# CHAPTER 4
# INTERNATIONAL BASKETBALL

In the first years of his career, Kobe did not see much international action. He opted not to take part in the 2000 Olympics, because that was the same year he planned to get married. Additionally, Kobe decided not to take part in the 2002 FIBA World Championship, and could not play internationally the following year nor in 2006 because of surgery.

Finally, in 2007, he was able to sport the Team USA jersey as he helped lead the team to a 10-0 gold medal finish at the FIBA Americas Championship. During the tournament, he averaged 15.3 points, 2.9 assists, 2.0 rebounds, and 1.6 steals per game.

In 2008, in his first Olympic game, he scored 20 points and had 6 assists.

Ultimately, he helped the team to win the gold medal, beating Spain in the final, 118-107.

He also played in 2012, earning a second gold medal. However, following the London games, he announced they would be his last.

# CHAPTER 5
# EXCLUSIVE DRILLS AND EXERCISES USED BY KOBE BRYANT

*"I can't relate to lazy people. We don't speak the same language.
I don't understand you. I don't want to understand you."*
– Kobe Bryant

Narratives about **Kobe's work ethic and training often sound like urban legends.** He's been known to average 6 hours a day of training 6 days a week. In high school, he would force people to play one-on-one games up to 100 points. Shaquille O'Neal has walked in the gym seeing Kobe practice drills, all alone, without a ball. He'll force teammates to stay after practice so that he can practice moves on them. And he's known to wake up at ungodly early hours to get extra court work, conditioning work, and strength work in, before the team's full-length two-hour practices.

## A word about his diet

Like many athletes and people, Kobe used to be able to successfully subsist off of junk food. It didn't slow him down, and he burned off the calories. However, as he's gotten older, he's had to change his diet to include more nutrients, to keep him healthier for longer on the court. He eats 5-6 meals a day, and consumes plenty of calories. He pays close attention to getting enough protein in his diet; thus, he consumes a lot of chicken, tuna, nuts, and red meats. He also eats plenty of healthy grains and vegetables. His pregame meal is always the same: chicken, rice, and broccoli. According to Kobe, *"Strong diet is the key to building a strong body."*

# Strength Training

Kobe's strength training routines are geared to make him a more explosive and forceful athlete. He often starts with higher reps, and does higher weight at lower repetitions the more sets he does. He'll isolate body parts — chest, shoulders, back, legs, and arms — on separate days, with a variety of gym exercises. Heavy weight lifting and running are the secrets to Kobe's strength and health.

## Chest

Kobe's chest exercises generally include:

- *Dumbbell Press, Incline* – 5 sets of 12, 10, 8, 6, 4 repetitions

- *Dumbbell Bench Press* – 5 sets of 12, 10, 8, 6, 4 repetitions
- *Cable Crossover* – 4 sets of 12 repetitions
- *Push-ups superset with Crossovers* – 4 sets of 15 repetitions

# Suicide Pushups

Kobe does a lot of push-ups. He says he can do 100 regular ones in a row, with relative ease. To make push-ups more difficult, Kobe is known to do something called suicide push-ups. This is when he launches himself up off the ground at the top of the push-up so both feet come up, then he will slap his hands against his chest. He will do 3 sets of 7 repetitions.

# Shoulders

- *Military Press Machine, Seated* – 3 sets of 21 repetitions
- *Dumbbell Lateral Raise superset with Dumbbell Front Raise* – 3 sets of 8 repetitions

- *Cable Raise, Rear Delts* – 5 sets of 12, 10, 8, 6, 4 repetitions
- *Hammer Shrug* – 5 sets of 12, 10, 8, 6, 4 repetitions

- *Four-way Neck Machine* – 4 sets of 12 repetitions

# Back

- *Lat Pulldown, Wide Grip* – 5 sets of 12, 10, 8, 6, 4 repetitions

- *Lat Pulldown, Close Grip* – 5 sets of 12, 10, 8, 6, 4 repetitions
- *Seated Row Machine, One Arm* – 4 sets of 12 repetitions

- *Back Extension* – 4 sets of 15, 15, 12, 12 repetitions

# Legs

- *Leg Press – 4 sets of 25, 20, 18, 16 repetitions*
- *Smith Machine Lunge – 4 sets of 8 repetitions for each leg*

- *Lying Leg Curl – 4 sets of 12, 10, 8, 6 repetitions*

- *Calf Raise, Standing – 6 sets of 16 repetitions*

# Arms

- *Dumbbell Curl, Alternating* – 5 sets of 12, 10, 8, 6, 4 repetitions

- *Preacher Machine Curl* – 6 sets of 12, 10, 8, 6, 21, 21 repetitions

- *Cable Triceps Extension* – 5 sets of 12, 10, 8, 6, 20 repetitions

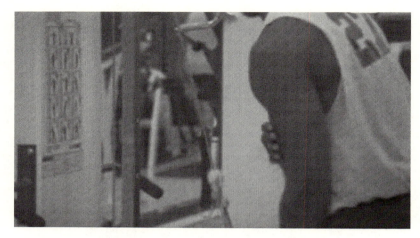

- *Cable Extension, Overhead* – 4 sets of 12, 10, 8, 20 repetitions
- *One-Arm Triceps Extension, Reverse Grip* – 2 sets of 15 repetitions

# Basketball Drills

Kobe spends two hours a day working on his game on the court. **On a daily basis, he *makes*, not takes, between 700-1000 shots**. There are five designated spots on the court from where he shoots. After making ten of them, he moves to a new location, stepping further away from the basket. In the midst of making all these shots, he does a series of job steps, one dribble pull-ups, and other moves.

## Mid-Post Drill

In this drill, someone passes Kobe the ball at the mid-post. He'll do a series of moves from here – a turn-around jump shot over both shoulders; he'll fake, take a dribble, and fade way; and he'll spin and drive to make a reverse layup. Often, they will add a defender so he gets into the habit of reading the defense.

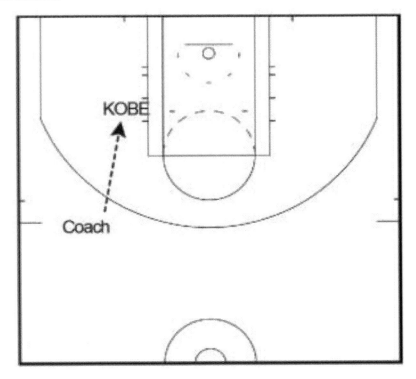

# Down Screen to Slip

Kobe's excellence at one-on-one games, especially from the wing, has made defenders keenly aware, and they try to prevent him from being able to drive from the side. Thus, Kobe has practiced slipping backdoor for a layup as they over-anticipate his retrieval on the wing. In the drill, they'll put a cone or a chair about 20 feet from the basket. Kobe starts at the block and pretends someone is coming down to set a screen for him to pop out. After an exaggerated fake, he'll sprint to the wing to receive the pass, then make a sharp backdoor cut for a pass underneath the basket. Then he'll lay it in or dunk the ball.

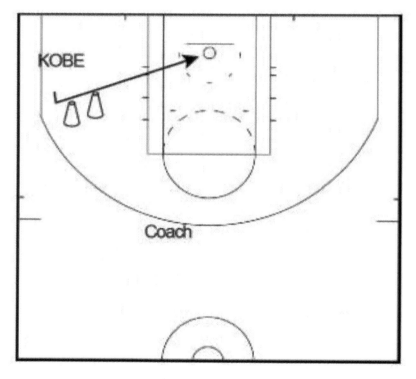

## Pick and Roll drill

Kobe is one of the best players to guard off the pick and roll. To practice, he sets up a chair or cone at the top of the key. He'll head in one direction, then come across the pick and drive towards the basket. From here, he'll do a repetition of a series of moves – he'll pull up for a jump shot; he'll do a hesitate-and-go, where he slows up to ease the defender, then hesitates and drives explosively; and finally, he'll slow down the defense, cross over, and continue to the basket.

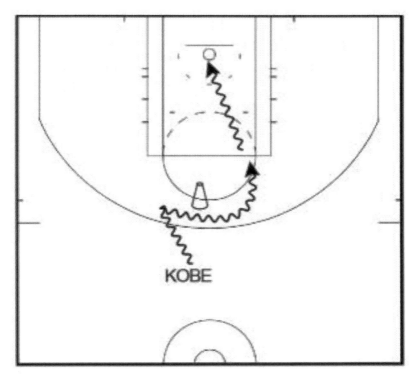

## Crossover Behind-the-Back Dribbling

In one dribbling drill, Kobe bounces back and forth, left to right, while alternating between a crossover and a behind-the-back dribble. This practices not only ball-handling, but changing direction and explosiveness.

## Crossover, Between the Legs, Behind the Back

Adding two new elements to the previous drill, Kobe will follow up by adding between the legs. He'll do a full crossover, left and back to right, followed by a between-the-legs dribble. After he throws the ball through his legs, he'll immediately throw it behind his back to the initial hand.

# Defensive Drills

Kobe has become one of the best players in history and not just because of his scoring and offensive play. He is also a terrific defender. He has **three basic tips** that have led to his defensive success.

1. *Stay Balanced*

    Kobe explains that many young players turn their torsos when they are learning to play defense. However, he says this is wrong. *"Now when your man changes direction, it takes too much time for you (to change direction) and slide. Everybody needs to think about staying in the middle. Your top part shouldn't be moving."*

2. *Keep your Hands Moving*

    Despite the importance of being quick on your feet and having a strong defensive stance, you won't go very far unless your hands are also acting to get in the offensive player's way. *"You have to keep your hands active, all the time. Up, down, side to side, jabbing at the ball,"* Kobe says.

3. *Maintain a Wide Base*

    Kobe puts it simply, *"If you keep your feet further apart, you have a wider base so your man can't change direction. I keep my wide base, and if you change direction, I'm still with you."*

These are some defensive drills that Kobe does to practice these three principles.

## Defensive Slide Drill

In this basic drill, Kobe will simply slide back and forth between the lines of key. When he gets to each side, he'll slam down his hands and hit the floor, and then slide in the opposite direction to the other line. This practices explosiveness, change of direction, and staying low.

## Sprint-and-Recover Defensive Drill

In this drill, one of Kobe's teammates will start in the corner of the floor. He'll be on the same baseline at the elbow. After his teammate starts dribbling, as if to drive for a fast break, he will sprint to catch up to him and slow him down. From there, he'll defend the one-on-one situation.

## Turn the Dribbler Drill

This drill is also done with a teammate. The offensive player's objective is to get to the other side of the court. Kobe's, or the defender's, objective is to make them change direction as many times as possible. This often means beating the player to the spot and making him alter his plan.

# CHAPTER 6
# PERSONAL LIFE, BUSINESS, AND PHILANTHROPY

## Personal Life

When Kobe was just twenty-one years old, he began working on a musical album. A seventeen-year-old, Vanessa Laine, attracted his attention as a background dancer. After only six months of dating, the two became engaged.

The two married on April 18, 2001, and gained media attention mainly because Kobe's parents were not in attendance. They opposed the marriage because they were young and, allegedly, because she was not African-American.

In 2002, the Bryants bought a $4 million house in Newport Beach, California. This occurred during the two-year stretch when Kobe did not speak to his parents. However, when Vanessa gave birth to their first daughter, Natalia Diamante Bryant, in 2003, his parents re-entered their lives.

Kobe still has two older sisters – Sharia and Shayla. Right now, he and his family live in California.

## Sexual Assault

If Kobe thought he experienced media scrutiny in the past, the threshold he would have to maintain would be severely tested in 2003. Over the summer, when he was staying in Colorado the night before a surgery, he had sex with a woman at the hotel. She claimed that he raped her, and a very public case was opened.

The woman's story had a number of inconsistent story lines. She showed up to the rape exam and the underpants she was wearing contained some other man's pubic hair and semen. She tried to dismiss this inconsistency, saying that she grabbed the wrong pair of underwear, but had previously claimed that she had not changed or showered after the incident. It was also revealed that she had attempted suicide in the past and had been treated for schizophrenia around the same time as the incident, weakening her case. The point in question was that her blood was found on Kobe's t-shirt, which was never fully hashed out.

Ultimately, the charges against Kobe were dropped because she refused to testify. Kobe was very much under the spotlight during 2003-2004 as a result of the case. Just a few weeks after being charged, he held a press conference as Vanessa sat at his side. He admitted to having sex with another woman – committing adultery – but claimed it was consensual.

After the charges were dropped, he came out and said:

*"First, I want to apologize directly to the young woman involved in this incident. I want to apologize to her for my behavior that night and for the consequences she has suffered in the past year. Although this year has been incredibly difficult for me personally, I can only imagine the pain she has had to endure. I also want to apologize to her parents and family members, and to my family and friends and supporters, and to the citizens of Eagle, Colorado.*

*I also want to make it clear that I do not question the motives of this young woman. No money has been paid to this woman. She has agreed that this statement will not be used against me in the civil case. Although I truly believe this encounter between us was consensual, I recognize now that she did not and does not view this incident the same way I did. After months of reviewing discovery, listening to her attorney, and even her testimony in person, I now understand how she feels that she did not consent to this encounter.*

*I issue this statement today fully aware that while one part of this case ends today, another remains. I understand that the civil case against me will go forward. That part of this case will be decided by and between the parties directly involved in the incident and will no longer be a financial or emotional drain on the citizens of the state of Colorado."*

Kobe had been dropped by a number of sponsors during the fiasco, which soon came back to him when he was presumed to be innocent by the greater public. He ended up signing a seven-year, $136 million contract in the NBA, and Nike, Spalding, and Coca-Cola sought to reinstate his contracts.

After a miscarriage in 2005, the couple gave birth to their second daughter – Gianna Maria-Onore Bryant – in 2006. In 2011, Vanessa Bryant filed for a divorce, however, by 2013, they publicly announced that they would remain together after solving their issues.

## Business

Kobe has had a great number of endorsement deals throughout his career. Before his life as a professional athlete even began, he signed a 6-year contract with Adidas worth $48 million. He also had endorsements with Coca-Cola (where he became the spokesperson for Sprite), and he had partnerships with McDonald's, Spalding, Upper Deck (an Italian chocolate company), and Nintendo.

Right before the sexual assault allegations, Nike had signed him to a 5-year $40-45 million contract, but refrained from promoting his image for two years. Of course, they did so once the dust settled. He has been the cover athlete for a number of basketball video games and been in commercials for a variety of video games, including the following:

- Kobe Bryant in the NBA Courtside
- NBA Courtside 2: Featuring Kobe Bryant
- NBA Courtside 2002
- NBA 3 on 3 Featuring Kobe Bryant
- NBA '07: Featuring the Life Vol. 2
- NBA '09: The Inside
- NBA 2K10

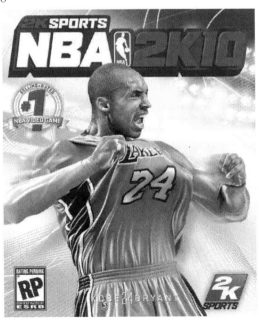

Kobe also partnered with Nubeo in 2009 to promote sports watches within the "Black Mamba Collection." They are named after him – his self-inscribed nickname being the Black Mamba. The watches run from $25,000 - $285,000.

In 2010, Kobe signed a deal with Turkish Airlines. He appeared in a promotional video for the company with Lionel Messi, which was aired in over 80 countries.

Estimates from CNN have indicated that Kobe likely rakes in $16 million a year from endorsement deals alone. This puts him behind athletes like Michael Jordan and Tiger Woods, Lionel Messi, and a few other superstars, on the *Forbes* list of highest paid athletes in the world.

Finally, Kobe established Kobe, Inc., with a headquarters in Newport Beach, California. BodyArmor sports drink was the first product he invested in. He is planning on investing in a variety of companies after retirement.

# Faith & Spirituality

Kobe was raised Roman Catholic and still practices today. He has expressed his faith in God outright, saying, *"I've pretty much done all I can here and, you know, God will carry me the rest of the way, so I'm pretty comfortable with that."*

Although Kobe is religious, he does not make religious statements quite as often as many other athletes. He has made statements saying that he would be open-minded to other faiths if the situation presented itself; although, that has yet to happen.

# Philanthropy

Kobe is affiliated with the After-School All-Stars (ASAS) and acts as the official ambassador. The non-profit organization offers programs to children in thirteen different cities.

Kobe also has a partnership with the Ching Ling Foundation after starting the Kobe Bryant China Fund. Money from the funds is used for charities in China that are focused on education and health.

Finally, Kobe and Zach Braff publicly donated $1 million to the Call of Duty Endowment, which is focused on helping veterans find career opportunities after military service.

# CHAPTER 7
# HIS FEARS AND SUPERSTITIONS

## Fears

Kobe has been known to declare his fearlessness in most interviews. He claims to not be afraid of nearly everything, especially if it relates at all to basketball and failure in any way. That said, there are things that give him a bit of the jitters.

### *Bees*

Kobe Bryant has said he is afraid of one thing: bees. This is fair, because he's allergic to them.

### *Dog S\*\*\**

This might seem a bit dramatic, but Kobe does everything he can to steer clear of dog poop. Despite having four dogs of his own, it creeps him out a bit. He associates the poop with a memory of living in Italy. He was wearing brand new "fresh" Nike shoes – the elephant print Jordans – and he stepped in a huge pile of dog poop. Since then, he fears the substance.

# Superstitions

## *Chewing his jersey*

Many have observed that Kobe has a somewhat unhygienic habit of chewing on his jersey during games. It looks like an act of nervousness, perhaps a superstition. The superstar claims it is a gross little trick his father taught him to cure thirst – sucking one's sweat out of his own jersey. However, many still speculate the full truth to this comment.

## *The story behind number: 8 to 24*

When Kobe was drafted, he chose the number 8. His first high school number, before switching to 33, was 24. That was the number he initially wanted, however, both 33 and 24 were unavailable upon entering the league. Number 24 was taken, and 33 was retired under Kareem Abdul-Jabbar. At the Adidas ABCD camp, he wore the number 143. Thus, when he added the digits together, he got 8 – and chose his number accordingly.

However, at the start of the 2006-2007 season, Kobe changed his number from 8 to 24. This came after a rough loss to the Phoenix Suns in the playoffs. Thus, the number switch indicated that Kobe was looking for more than a simple jersey switch – he was looking for a serious change. He told some reporters from TNT that it was also supposed to indicate hard work, because 24 is the number of hours in a day and the amount that he dedicates to basketball.

In many ways, too, his number change can be read as a personality change. Number 8 was the number he wore when he first entered the league and gained the reputation of being an immature, albeit talented, but cocky and ungrateful athlete. Later in his career, he became known to be much more humble and appreciative of his opportunities. In many ways, it could be seen as an identity shift.

Finally, others have speculated that he did so to claim more of an ownership of his accomplishments. Number 8 was the number he wore with Shaquille O'Neal and Phil Jackson – very big names – whereas, number 24 is much more his own. There is no doubt that Kobe's number will be retired, but which one it will be is still open to discussion.

# CHAPTER 8
# TOP 8 MOTIVATIONAL LESSONS FROM KOBE BRYANT

1. **Don't Be Afraid to Play with Rage**

   *"Once I discovered (letting my emotions erupt on the basketball court), everything about the game changed. Because now I understood that I could really lose myself through the game. And no matter what affected me, no matter what happened in life. I could always step on to the court and just absolutely erupt. The feeling of playing with that rage was new to me, but I f\*\*ing loved it."*

2. **Make Sacrifices**

   *"There's a choice that we have to make as people as individuals. If you want to be great at something there is a choice you have to make. We can all be masters at our craft, but you have to make a choice. What I mean by that is, there are inherent sacrifices that come along with that, family time, hanging out with your friends, being a great friend, being a great son, nephew, whatever the case may be. There are sacrifices that come along with making that decision."*

3. **Embrace Doubt**

   *"I have moments and I have days where I doubt myself. But to me, that's the exciting part of the challenge. That's when I realize this is a great opportunity to come out and show everybody this is how you bounce back. This is how you respond to a challenge."*

4. **Never Stop Learning**

   *"It's really about wanting to learn and feeling like your cup is always empty, because there's always more that you can fill with it. That's the really important thing and just continuing to learn, learn, learn."*

5. **Focus**

   *"No matter what you do, if you want to be a basketball player, if you want to be a writer if you want to be a TV host, or whatever it is that you want to do. It's making sure that you focus with laser-like precision on that goal and you learn from oth-*

er people who have been great. Because no matter what they're doing there's always a common thread, there's always a common denominator between what has made people great and what has separated good from great."

6. **Put all your effort in it**

    *"It's the ultimate. The fans recognizing the hard work I'm putting on the court... It's a great honor."* It teaches you that you will be noticed if you put enough effort into something.

7. **Let the past go**

    *"I look at tonight like a learning experience, I just want to be the best basketball player I can be."* It encourages letting the past go and looking forward to the future.

8. **Don't be afraid to work hard**

    *"Hard work pays off."* Hard work will eventually pay off; just look at the beginning of Kobe's life through the end of his career, and you will realize how much he's gone through.

# CHAPTER 9
# FAMOUS PEOPLE INSPIRED BY KOBE

### - Jason Kidd
*"Kobe was great. He practices as if it's Game 7. He wants to prove that he's the best player in the world every single practice."*

### - Shaquille O'Neal
*"Kobe is a scientific dawg. He works out every day, practices every day. Most of the other stars are just dawgs, not scientific dawgs.*

*Me, I'm a freak-of-nature dawg because of my size. LeBron could be a scientific dawg like Kobe, but he's not, he's got a lot going on like I did, so that's preventing him from being one."*

### - Jim Boeheim (Coach of USA Olympic team)
*"Kobe, from day one, is just the hardest-working player I've ever been around. He just does an unbelievable job. He came in, he worked out before practice and practiced harder than anybody and then worked out afterwards and continued the whole trip. The first trip we are qualifying and then the Olympics themselves.*

*He's just an unbelievable competitor and goes 100 percent every day in practice and that brings everybody else up to that same level. He was a huge part of us being ready in the Olympics to be able to win. Of course, when we needed a big shot, he made a big shot against Spain."*

### - Kevin Durant
*"We had the day off, but they said we could get some shots up if we wanted, so I decided to head over with [Oklahoma City teammate and Team USA hopeful] Jeff Green.*

*Kobe [Bryant] was the only guy on the bus, and that spoke volumes to me – he's the best player in the game, yet he's always willing to come work on his game, so that kind of motivated me and Jeff.*

*He went by himself, he got a lot of shots up, and by the time he was done you could see he* had gotten better over that hour. Like I said, it was a big inspiration to me and Jeff."

**- Jerry West (Lakers Manager)**

*"What's most impressive about this young man are his desire, his work ethic, his competitive nature. [Bryant] comes to the arena at 4:30, before anybody is here, and works on his game alone. He has incredible skills and the desire to be a great player.*

*We're extremely happy with Kobe's development – and we think he's going to keep improving. You haven't seen the best of Kobe yet."*

**- Larry Drew (Assistant Lakers coach)**

*"I was surprised and shocked by his skill level, but I was more amazed by Kobe's level of confidence, a kid coming out of high school."*

**- Adidas**

*"Kobe is a kid with a vision, a kid with a dream."*

**- Michael Jordan**

*"I see a lot of myself in him. No doubt about it."*

**- Del Harris (Former Lakers coach)**

*"Nobody can guard Kobe one-on-one. Nobody."*

**- Alvin Gentry (NBA coach)**

*"I've always thought he was the best player in basketball. I don't think it's even close."*

**- Phil Jackson (Lakers head coach)**

*"He's learned how to become a leader in a way in which people want to follow him. That's really important for him to have learned that because he knew that he had to give to get back in return, and so he's become a giver rather than just a guy that's a demanding leader. That's been great for him and great to watch."*

# CHAPTER 10
# KOBE'S BASKETBALL PHILOSOPHY

In his twenty years of playing professional basketball, Kobe has seen it all. For all his successes, he has had as many failures and has learned from them. Here are some insights into his philosophy on how to play the game – both physically and mentally.

Kobe Bryant holds several NBA shooting and scoring records, which explains why he is often called one of the NBA's most "dangerous" scorers. He is recorded as making the most three-pointers in a single game (12), and he has scored 81 points in a single game, which makes his performance the second highest in league history. Four different times, he averaged 40 points in a calendar month – the third player in the NBA to do so. Kobe, like Michael Jordan, earned recognition by shooting a *fall-away jump shot*.

*Sports Illustrated* writer Chris Ballard has described another well-known Bryant move as the **"jab step-and-pause."** This is where Kobe will jab his non-pivot foot forward, allowing the defender to relax. Then, rather than bringing back the jab foot, he pushes off of it and drives around his opponent to reach the basket.

## Don't Be Afraid of Failure

For all his amazing scoring performances and scoring records, Kobe has missed a lot of shots. In 2014, Kobe broke the record for the most missed shots. In an interview, when asked if he was upset about this, he responded:

*"No, because I've failed before, and I woke up the next morning, and I'm OK. People say bad things about you in the paper on Monday, and then on Wednesday, you're the greatest thing since sliced bread. I've seen that cycle, so why would I be nervous about it happening?"*

Part of the key to Kobe's success has been taking risky shots and risking failure. In fact, in his career, Kobe has missed more basket attempts than any other NBA player ever. Ultimately, he believes you must take risks and fail to succeed on the highest level.

## Stay Calm

Especially in intense postseason games, Kobe has learned that getting too excited is not ideal. While athletes need to be excited to get out there and give it their all, maintaining a sense of composure is of the utmost importance. Kobe has seen it in himself and his teammates in important games; the first quarter can be sloppy and unproductive as players try to do too much. While realizing that the stakes are heightened, to a certain extent, Kobe believes it needs to be treated like any other game.

## Move the Ball

Even in Kobe's highest scoring games, he is a firm believer that ball movement is critical to success. He has one of the most impressive repertoires of moves and, in his prime, could frequently score against anyone, regardless of how well they could anticipate his next steps.

Swinging the ball from one side of the court to the other side of the court opens up the defense and allows for more opportunity. It spreads the defense out so he can't collapse on others.

## Move on to the Next Play

Kobe has said that he hates basically nothing more than turnovers. They drive him crazy, especially when he is the one responsible. Despite this, he doesn't allow himself to dwell on any play. Whether it was a turnover, a missed open shot, etc. He has said the important thing to do is forget about it and move on.

## Work on your Defense

Aside from Kobe's offense capabilities, he is also credited as being a noteworthy defender; especially, since he earned a position on the All-Defensive team twelve times. Kobe infrequently performs violations or fouls while playing defense. He believes this level of caution and thought has contributed to his longevity by sparing physical damage to his body.

# CHAPTER 11
# 15 INTERESTING FACTS YOU DIDN'T KNOW ABOUT KOBE BRYANT

1. In the off-season, Kobe will develop new moves by treating his shadow as a defender.
2. Kobe has said his favorite player growing up was Mike D'Antoni, who also wore number 8.
3. Kobe is named after a type of steak.
4. In high school, Kobe was a member of a rap group called CHEIZAW. They were later signed by Sony Entertainment.

5. Kobe was named high school player of the year. He scored more than 2,000 points in high school, and he could dunk the ball in the 8th grade.
6. When Kobe first spoke to Michael Jordan, he said, "You know I can kick your a** one-on-one."

7. Growing up, Kobe was a big fan of the game Double Dribble. He played big tournaments with his relatives at his grandmother's house.

8. Coach Harris, the first Lakers coach in Kobe's career, didn't put him in because he thought he wouldn't fit in the offense.
9. Bryant gave himself the nickname "Black Mamba." He wanted to embody the animal on the court as the snake has the ability to "strike with 99% accuracy."
10. During 2012-2013, he started to nickname himself "vino" because he believed he was aging well, like wine.
11. Shaquille O'Neal was rapping while free-styling at a NYC club about Kobe's failures. He calls him out for losing in the playoffs and for ratting on him about cheating on his wife. Kobe pretended it doesn't bother him.
12. In 2006, just six minutes before Shaquille O'Neal's daughter, Kobe's daughter, Gianna Maria-Onore, was born.
13. Growing up, his favorite television program was NBA Showmen.
14. In 2008, he asked Nike to shave a few millimeters from the bottom of his shoes in order to get reaction time that was a hundredth of a second better.
15. ESPN ranked Kobe as the second greatest shooting guard of all time, in 2007, after Michael Jordan. Which is who Kobe is often compared to and who inspired his playing style. In that same year, TNT and Sporting News named Kobe the player of the 2000s (specifically, that first decade).

# KOBE BRYANT

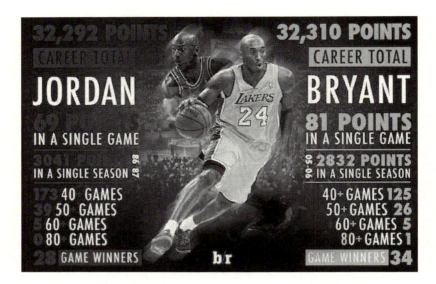

# CHAPTER 12
# AWARDS AND RECOGNITION

Kobe is the youngest player in NBA history (starting at 17 years old), and to play in the All-Star Game (at 19 years old), and also the youngest player to make it to the NBA Finals (aged 21). On top of that, he's the youngest player to reach 10,000, all the way to 20,000 and 30,000, points respectively! The Black Mamba is known as one of the best players in the clutch (end). He is third on the NBA's all-time regular season and all-time postseason scoring lists and twice led the league for scoring. Kobe has won the most All-Star MVP Awards (4) in NBA history.

Below are all of his awards and achievements throughout his career.

## 2014-2015
- NBA All Star

## 2013-2014
- NBA All Star

## 2012-2013
- All-NBA 1st Team
- NBA All Star

## 2011-2012
- All-NBA 1st Team
- All-Defensive 2nd Team
- Olympic Gold Medal
- NBA All Star

## 2010-2011
- NBA All-Star Game MVP
- All-NBA 1st Team
- All-Defensive 1st Team
- ESPY – Best NBA Player Award
- NBA All Star

## 2009-2010
- NBA Champion
- NBA Finals MVP
- All-NBA 1st Team
- All-Defensive 1st Team
- ESPY – Best NBA Player Award
- NBA All Star

## 2008-2009
- NBA Champion
- NBA Finals MVP
- All-NBA 1st Team
- All-Defensive 1st Team

- NBA All-Star Game MVP
- NBA All Star

## 2007-2008
- NBA Champion
- NBA MVP
- All-NBA 1st Team
- All-Defensive 1st Team
- ESPY – Best NBA Player Award
- Olympic Gold Medal
- NBA All Star

## 2006-2007
- NBA Scoring Champion
- All-NBA 1st Team
- NBA All-Star Game MVP
- 2007 FIBA Americas Championship
- NBA All Star

## 2005-2006
- NBA Scoring Champion
- All-NBA 1st Team
- All-Defensive 1st Team
- Under Armour Undeniable Performance Award
- NBA All Star

## 2004-2005
- All-NBA 3rd Team
- NBA All Star

## 2003-2004
- All-NBA 1st Team
- All-Defensive 1st Team

- NBA All Star

## 2002-2003
- All-NBA 1st Team
- All-Defensive 1st Team
- ESPY – Outstanding Team Award
- NBA All Star

## 2001-2002
- NBA Champion
- NBA All-Star Game MVP
- All-NBA 1st Team
- All-Defensive 2nd Team
- ESPY – Outstanding Team Award
- NBA All Star

## 2000-2001
- NBA Champion
- All-NBA 2nd Team
- All-Defensive 2nd Team
- NBA All Star

## 1999-2000
- NBA Champion
- All-NBA 2nd Team
- All-Defensive 1st Team
- NBA All Star

## 1998-1999
- All-NBA 3rd Team

## 1997-1998
- NBA All Star

## 1996-1997
- NBA Slam Dunk Champion

## 1995-1996
- Naismith High School Player of the Year
- 1996 Gatorade Circle of Champions High School Player of the Year
- McDonald's High School All-American
- USA Today All-USA First Team
- USA Today National High School Player of the Year
- PARADE National High School Player of the Year
- Adidas Academic Betterment and Career Development Summer Camp Senior MVP

# CHAPTER 13
# NBA SEASON STATS

| Legend | | | | | |
|---|---|---|---|---|---|
| GP | Games played | GS | Games started | MPG | Minutes per game |
| FG% | Field goal percentage | 3P% | 3-point field goal percentage | FT% | Free throw percentage |
| RPG | Rebounds per game | APG | Assists per game | SPG | Steals per game |
| BPG | Blocks per game | PPG | Points per game | Bold | Career high |

| | |
|---|---|
| † | Denotes seasons in which Bryant won an NBA championship |
| * | Led the league |

## Regular Season Statistics

| Year | Team | GP | GS | MPG | FG% | 3P% | FT% | RPG | APG | SPG | BPG | PPG |
|---|---|---|---|---|---|---|---|---|---|---|---|---|
| 1996–97 | L.A. Lakers | 71 | 6 | 15.5 | .417 | .375 | .819 | 1.9 | 1.3 | .7 | .3 | 7.6 |
| 1997–98 | L.A. Lakers | 79 | 1 | 26.0 | .428 | .341 | .794 | 3.1 | 2.5 | .9 | .5 | 15.4 |
| 1998–99 | L.A. Lakers | 50 | 50 | 37.9 | .465 | .267 | .839 | 5.3 | 3.8 | 1.4 | **1.0** | 19.9 |
| 1999–00† | L.A. Lakers | 66 | 62 | 38.2 | .468 | .319 | .821 | 6.3 | 4.9 | 1.6 | .9 | 22.5 |
| 2000–01† | L.A. Lakers | 68 | 68 | 40.9 | .464 | .305 | .853 | 5.9 | 5.0 | 1.7 | .6 | 28.5 |
| 2001–02† | L.A. Lakers | 80 | 80 | 38.3 | **.469** | .250 | .829 | 5.5 | 5.5 | 1.5 | .4 | 25.2 |
| 2002–03 | L.A. Lakers | **82** | **82** | 41.5 | .451 | **.383** | .843 | **6.9** | 5.9 | **2.2** | .8 | 30.0 |
| 2003–04 | L.A. Lakers | 65 | 64 | 37.6 | .438 | .327 | .852 | 5.5 | 5.1 | 1.7 | .4 | 24.0 |
| 2004–05 | L.A. Lakers | 66 | 66 | 40.7 | .433 | .339 | .816 | 5.9 | 6.0 | 1.3 | .8 | 27.6 |
| 2005–06 | L.A. Lakers | 80 | 80 | 41.0 | .450 | .347 | .850 | 5.3 | 4.5 | 1.8 | .4 | **35.4\*** |
| 2006–07 | L.A. Lakers | 77 | 77 | 40.8 | .463 | .344 | **.868** | 5.7 | 5.4 | 1.4 | .5 | 31.6\* |
| 2007–08 | L.A. Lakers | **82** | **82** | 38.9 | .459 | .361 | .840 | 6.3 | 5.4 | 1.8 | .5 | 28.3 |
| 2008–09† | L.A. Lakers | **82** | **82** | 36.1 | .467 | .351 | .856 | 5.2 | 4.9 | 1.5 | .5 | 26.8 |
| 2009–10† | L.A. Lakers | 73 | 73 | 38.8 | .456 | .329 | .811 | 5.4 | 5.0 | 1.5 | .3 | 27.0 |
| 2010–11 | L.A. Lakers | **82** | **82** | 33.9 | .451 | .323 | .828 | 5.1 | 4.7 | 1.2 | .1 | 25.3 |
| 2011–12 | L.A. Lakers | 58 | 58 | 38.5 | .430 | .303 | .845 | 5.4 | 4.6 | 1.2 | .3 | 27.9 |
| 2012–13 | L.A. Lakers | 78 | 78 | 38.6 | .463 | .324 | .839 | 5.6 | 6.0 | 1.4 | .3 | 27.3 |
| 2013–14 | L.A. Lakers | 6 | 6 | 29.5 | .425 | .188 | .857 | 4.3 | **6.3** | 1.2 | .2 | 13.8 |
| 2014–15 | L.A. Lakers | 35 | 35 | 34.5 | .373 | .293 | .813 | 5.7 | 5.6 | 1.3 | .2 | 22.3 |
| 2015–16 | L.A. Lakers | 66 | 66 | 28.2 | .358 | .285 | .826 | 3.7 | 2.8 | .9 | .2 | 17.6 |
| Career | | 1,346 | 1,198 | 36.1 | .447 | .329 | .837 | 5.2 | 4.7 | 1.4 | .5 | 25.0 |
| All-Star | | 15 | 15 | 27.6 | .500 | .324 | .789 | 5.0 | 4.7 | 2.5 | .4 | 19.3 |

## Playoffs Statistics

| Year | Team | GP | GS | MPG | FG% | 3P% | FT% | RPG | APG | SPG | BPG | PPG |
|---|---|---|---|---|---|---|---|---|---|---|---|---|
| 1997 | L.A. Lakers | 9 | 0 | 14.8 | .382 | .261 | .867 | 1.2 | 1.2 | .3 | .2 | 8.2 |
| 1998 | L.A. Lakers | 11 | 0 | 20.0 | .408 | .214 | .689 | 1.9 | 1.5 | .3 | .7 | 8.7 |
| 1999 | L.A. Lakers | 8 | 8 | 39.4 | .430 | .348 | .800 | 6.9 | 4.6 | **1.9** | 1.3 | 19.8 |
| 2000† | L.A. Lakers | 22 | 22 | 39.0 | .442 | .344 | .754 | 4.5 | 4.4 | 1.5 | **1.5** | 21.1 |
| 2001† | L.A. Lakers | 16 | 16 | 43.4 | .469 | .324 | .821 | **7.3** | **6.1** | 1.6 | .8 | 29.4 |
| 2002† | L.A. Lakers | 19 | 19 | 43.8 | .434 | .379 | .759 | 5.8 | 4.6 | 1.4 | .9 | 26.6 |
| 2003 | L.A. Lakers | 12 | 12 | 44.3 | .432 | **.403** | .827 | 5.1 | 5.2 | 1.2 | .1 | 32.1 |
| 2004 | L.A. Lakers | 22 | 22 | 44.2 | .413 | .247 | .813 | 4.7 | 5.5 | **1.9** | .3 | 24.5 |
| 2006 | L.A. Lakers | 7 | 7 | **44.9** | **.497** | .400 | .771 | 6.3 | 5.1 | 1.1 | .4 | 27.9 |
| 2007 | L.A. Lakers | 5 | 5 | 43.0 | .462 | .357 | **.919** | 5.2 | 4.4 | 1.0 | .4 | **32.8** |
| 2008 | L.A. Lakers | 21 | 21 | 41.1 | .479 | .302 | .809 | 5.7 | 5.6 | 1.7 | .4 | 30.1 |
| 2009† | L.A. Lakers | 23 | 23 | 40.8 | .457 | .349 | .883 | 5.3 | 5.5 | 1.7 | .9 | 30.2 |
| 2010† | L.A. Lakers | 23 | 23 | 40.1 | .458 | .374 | .842 | 6.0 | 5.5 | 1.3 | .7 | 29.2 |
| 2011 | L.A. Lakers | 10 | 10 | 35.4 | .446 | .293 | .820 | 3.4 | 3.3 | 1.6 | .3 | 22.8 |
| 2012 | L.A. Lakers | 12 | 12 | 39.7 | .439 | .283 | .832 | 4.8 | 4.3 | 1.3 | .2 | 30.0 |
| | Career | 220 | 200 | 39.3 | .448 | .331 | .816 | 5.1 | 4.7 | 1.4 | .6 | 25.6 |

# CONCLUSION

Kobe Bryant's legacy will be tremendous, both in the NBA and in society. He has challenged conventional notions of what devotion and hard training truly mean, and his impact will be felt for decades to come.

Understanding Kobe Bryant on a dynamic level is exceedingly difficult. He seems to operate on a plane different than almost everyone in the world, and his devotion to a private lifestyle makes this understanding all the more difficult.

However, attempting to uncover the secrets and strategies to his success and achievements are still duly important. Having grown up in the spotlight and cast in the shadow of Michael Jordan when he was still a teenager, Kobe has undergone tremendous development.

Though he is retiring, the memory of his skills, tactics, mind-set, and work ethic, will remain, and he will not soon be forgotten.

# ABOUT THE AUTHOR

Steve James isn't your typical sports fan. While there are some that will always make time to watch the big game, James started following the NBA at a very young age and has watched some of the best players in the history of the NBA from the very beginning. Even at that young age, he started paying attention to who was really standing out on the court – greats like Michael Jordan, Magic Johnson, or Larry Bird. Steve follows the game to this day and knows the ins and outs of the greatest NBA stars of today, like Kobe Bryant, LeBron James, Kevin Durant, or Stephen Curry. Having carefully watched these players on the court and studied their lives, he has a unique perspective into their success, how it was achieved, and what makes them so great.

He has an insider view into the secrets that have made these players so successful. By collecting this information into his books, he hopes to help not just young, aspiring basketball players, but all people to learn the secrets of what it takes to be successful. By looking at how these players have reached their goals, the readers will glean the information they need to reach their own goals. Steve's years of analyzing play styles, successes, failures, training routines, etc. gives him a real insight into these players!

Made in the USA
Middletown, DE
11 February 2020